VEHICLES ON THE JOB

DUMP TRUCKS

ON THE CONSTRUCTION SITE

by Samantha Bell

Cherry Lake Press

Published in the United States of America
by Cherry Lake Publishing
Ann Arbor, Michigan
www.cherrylakepublishing.com

Reading Adviser: Beth Walker Gambro, MS, Ed., Reading Consultant, Yorkville, IL
Content Adviser: Louis Teel, Professor of Heavy Equipment Operating, Central Arizona College

Photo Credits: © Reyhan Reynardot/Shutterstock, MuhammadAbdulJalil01/Shutterstock, cover, title page; © Mr. Tempter/Shutterstock, 4; © Edvision/Shutterstock, 6; © AYDO8/Shutterstock, 8; © GKV/iStock.com, 10; © dgmata/Shutterstock, 12; © HenadziPechan/Shutterstock, 14; © Teamjackson/iStock.com, 16; © RobSt/Shutterstock, 18; © vovashevchuk/iStock.com, 20

Cherry Lake Press is an imprint of Cherry Lake Publishing Group.

Library of Congress Cataloging-in-Publication Data has been filed and is available at catalog.loc.gov

Cherry Lake Press would like to acknowledge the work of the Partnership for 21st Century Learning, a Network of Battelle for Kids. Please visit Battelle for Kids online for more information.

Printed in the United States of America

Note from Publisher: Websites change regularly, and their future contents are outside of our control. Supervise children when conducting any recommended online searches for extended learning opportunities.

TABLE OF CONTENTS

MOVING MATERIALS

Dump trucks have **containers** on the back. The containers are called dump boxes.

They carry **materials** to the **construction site**. They carry materials away from it.

CONNECT

What other vehicles carry materials?

LIFTING LOADS

Some carry dirt or sand.
Some carry **gravel** or rocks.

Some carry construction **debris**. Some trucks can carry up to 100 tons!

LOOK

Look at the load in the dump truck. What debris is it taking away?

TIRES AND TERRAIN

Dump trucks have large tires. The tires can hold up the heavy loads.

Some trucks have 4 wheels.
Some have 6 or 8 wheels.
Some have 10 to 18 wheels!

THINK

Why do you think some dump trucks have more wheels than others?

The tires can go on soft, muddy ground. They can go on hard, rough ground.

GET THE JOB DONE!

A dump truck has lift **cylinders**. They push up one end of the dump box. The materials slide out.

Dump trucks keep things moving!

FIND OUT MORE

Go online with an adult to find videos of dump trucks. Write down some things you **see** and **hear**.

Then, write what you **think** about those things. **Make a connection** to something else you know.

Next, write what you **wonder** about dump trucks from the videos. What would you like to learn more about?

GLOSSARY

construction site (kuhn-STRUHK-shuhn SITE) the place where something was, is, or will be built

containers (kuhn-TAY-nerz) objects such as boxes, jars, or barrels that are used to hold something

cylinders (SIL-uhn-duhrz) long, round shapes with 2 flat circles on either end

debris (duh-BREE) the pieces that are left after something has been broken or destroyed

gravel (GRAV-uhl) small pieces of rock used on paths and roads

materials (muh-TEER-ee-uhlz) things you need for a project or activity

INDEX

ABOUT THE AUTHOR

Samantha Bell has written over 100 books for children. She lives in South Carolina with her family and pets.